# Granny Albyn's Complaint

Thanks are due to the editors of the following
publications where some of these poems first appeared
- *Cencrastus, Freedom Springs,
Poetry Scotland, Pulsar and Saw.*


'In history the end is closed: we know
what it is and can only be.
In art it is open:
it is what we make of it.'
(Christopher Hill, *The Experience of Defeat*)


'Without Contraries is no progression.'
(William Blake, *The Marriage of Heaven and Hell*)

# Granny Albyn's Complaint
David Betteridge

Published 2008 by
Smokestack Books
PO Box 408, Middlesbrough TS5 6WA
e-mail : info@smokestack-books.co.uk
www.smokestack-books.co.uk

**Granny Albyn's Complaint**
David Betteridge
Copyright 2008 David Betteridge, all rights reserved

Cover: detail from *Unfurling Our History - Our Future*
by Ken Currie (c) Glasgow City Council (Museums)

Printed by
EPW Print & Design Ltd

ISBN 978-0-9554028-3-8
Smokestack Books gratefully
acknowledges the support of
Middlesbrough Borough Council
and Arts Council North East

Smokestack Books is a member of
Independent Northern Publishers
www.northernpublishers.co.uk
and is represented by Inpress Ltd
www.inpressbooks.co.uk

# Contents

- 7 Open Sesame
- 8 A New Mask of Anarchy
- 9 Chorus of the Elites
- 10 Hellsayings
- 12 We Shall Obey
- 13 Auguries of Evil
- 15 Young Albyn's Plea
- 19 Tree, Bird, Fish, Bell
- 21 Carriers
- 23 On the Last (and Next) War
- 24 May Day: In Parenthesis
- 28 Unbending
- 29 Scorching
- 30 Seed-corn
- 31 Spiderlike
- 32 A Fish Rising
- 34 The People's Palace History Paintings
- 36 Fighting Back
- 37 In Brecht's Bar
- 38 Giving Back Riches
- 39 Granny Albyn's Complaint
- 42 Boogying
- 43 Various
- 44 Glasgow's Needleworks Project
- 46 Chorus of the Masses
- 47 Scum
- 48 May Day: Happy Returns
- 56 Bread and Book
- 57 Athene
- 58 The Net
- 59 Heavensayings
- 61 No Mean City
- 62 A Wishing Tree
- 63 Notes

# Open Sesame

*'Well grubbed, old mole!'*
Karl Marx


Under the furrows of old Europe
lay
the ruin and the saving
of its steady, backward way: coal,
coal upon coal.

Raging, rampant,
fired by this unhappy good,
the anarch Progress forced its change,
lavishly and all-consumingly, on every land
and every suffering folk
that came within the blight and blessing
of its rule of smoke.

Unimpeded by disablements of care,
within a century
the iron masters and their human tools
exhausted Europe,
then went on to wreak their marvel
on the other continents of looted Earth.

Their legacy to us:
they redefined and laid to ruthless rest
the past that they inherited,
and brought, heroically, our doomed dystopia
to the titan fury of its birth.

## A New Mask of Anarchy

I saw, as in a dream or one of Goya's caprichos,
the swelling triumph of the newly orthodox.
Their practised slogans echoed
from the West to East. Set free, their greed
rampaged. Their anarchy spread wide;
pundits praised it; publics danced
to its paltry tune.

I heard the voices of the rich usurp,
and spoil, the tenets of democracy.
I heard them lie to sanctify the contest -
never mind the losses or the pain - of each
against the rival ruck of each.

A bastille falls - ca ira! -
in Reason's name,
while new unReasons rise
to force on us their squalid reign.

# Chorus of the Elites
## Against the Masses

We see further,
want more, and fear less.
You, sunk in your toils,
make do, and work no change.

We, by way of hard-fought battlings,
taking risks, advance.
You share our superflux.

Did your millions, simultaneous and unled,
construct the wheel, tame fire,
and leave the dark proximity of caves?

Did you, on a sudden day,
pre-empt Pythagoras; or, enlightened,
sit with Buddha underneath his tree?

Did Bach or Shakespeare need your help?
Did Newton's apple fall on any of your heads?

When did you ever think to harness steam,
and make an Empire run?

You are the world's losers, our servants,
each epoch's scum.

# Hellsayings

*Words of Experience Spoken by Some Inhabitants of Purgatory*

1. Romantic poets and their readers hear a songbird carolling, and call it sweet. I hear a worm-filled killer insisting, *This is my patch. Keep your beak out.*

2. The gurgling baby that thinks itself adored by the whole world will learn its error soon enough.

3. Shopkeepers tell us, *What you see is what you get.* Normally, we get less.

4. *Know thou this, that men / Are as the time is.* That is what Shakespeare has his bastard Edmund say. It is true. It is also true that the present time is characterised by a prevalence of jungles and deserts, some real, most metaphorical.

5. Change rules; and rules change, except the one that enjoins, *Look after Number One.*

6. Shit happens; but take none. Give it, rather.

7. The world is my oyster. I crack it open in the hope of finding a fat, shining pearl, which I will sell to the highest bidder.

8. Don't be fooled by the conventional fiction that the Seven Capital Sins are deadly; they are not. They are not even sins. Take Pride, Avarice, and Wrath, for example. These are just hostile ways of describing and discouraging the virtues of Self-Respect, Wanting to Get On, and Sticking Up for Yourself.

9. *Love* is a fig-leaf of a term - a transparent one - behind which adolescents of all ages try to hide their infantile delusions and naked, needy ego. They fail, of course.

10. Be prepared to be disappointed.

11. Cursed are the peacemakers, for they shall be called weak.

12. Blessed are those that get in their tit before anyone else's tat, for they shall be called bold. To them, for their enterprise, falls the right to dispose of the world's riches.

# We Shall Obey

There is a cord, woven
from love and from the fear of loss
of love. It bonds us
to the worst, as to the best,
the past has given.

There is a warm familiar drug
in the half loaves we buy,
an opiate
that makes us meek.

There are lies concealed
in the home truths we learn
and teach our sons and daughters
to repeat.

At every turn,
to all the caring and repressive powers that be,
time and again, *Yes*, we say,
*whatever you wish. We shall obey.*

# Auguries of Evil

### Twins
I wander through the chequer
of our warring streets, where Wealth
and wealth's misuse, as old as Time,
run deep.
Every second face I see
bears marks of pain and hopelessness,
revealing Profit's poor essential twin,
Defeat.

### Addict
A young child cries, with piercing voice,
insistently, victim of a need
she cannot tell. Addict from the womb,
she gives her mother (prior victim,
user, pusher) little peace.
Her mother gives her desperate blows
that bruise, but do not quell,
with overtures of desperate kisses
intermixed.

### One of a horde
A beggar, one of a horde
as numerous as lamp posts, importunes.
Seated, skirted round with care in rags -
they make it seem he has no legs -
he reaches out, and, 'Any change to spare?'
he croaks, below waist height.
Few passers-by respond.
Most shrink from being drawn,
either through a look or word,
even for an instant, into any of his dirt.
His spittles shoot.
His brown encrusted lips work hard.
He argues to the empty air
against his tenancy of ever lower circles
in the hell that is his fate. Tonight,

as every night, unwashed, ill-nourished,
he will sleep outdoors, alone,
his head, to save it from the rain and wind,
encapsuled in a wooden crate.

**Lovers**
He twists and pushes, twists again efficiently,
and jerks. Her forearm breaks.
He smiles to know her pain,
and feel his power thus proved.
Puffed up, the youth walks on,
his humbling by the world since he was born
forgotten for a while.
She, his lover and forgiver, follows
with a space of fifty yards between.
Neither guesses she, within the year,
will be his killer.

# Young Albyn's Plea

Any change to spare?
Fuck off, then. Have a hellish day.
There's too much money in this town
in the wrong hands, not mine.

What's coming now? Here's posh!
The dress she's scarcely wearing must have cost a bomb.
It could have kept me
through last winter's cold.
Any change to spare?
Please, I'm going spare. No?
You stingy cow, you stingy, ugly, plastic cow!

And you, you with your staring eyes,
what are you doing, selling or buying?
Either way, no deal.
If you must stand there, stand to the side,
block out the breeze,
and let the sun shine warm on me.
(I'm a woman who likes her warm.)
But, better, go.

Now here's a mob of strutters strutting by.
Who do they think they are?
Who cares?
Change? Any change?
Not a bean.
Given half their wealth, I'd be as good and grand.
But no. Only the smallest of small change
is given.

If we want fair shares, we have to take.
Asking is a mug's game.
Mugging: now there's a healthier line.
It's more direct.

What, still staring with your staring eyes,
judging me, and sentencing?
Yes, guilty, as I've always been,
ever since the day that I was fool enough
to let myself be born.
Guilty of poor choices:
dead-end place and time of birth...
dodgy parents... schooling... the company I've kept...
the things I do... the things I do not do...
Wrong, all wrong!

What do you see, then, when you look at me?
Nothing, that is what:
an empty nought.
No, worse:
I am a nought that's full, brim-full
with emptiness
and the aching hell it brings.

If it's pity that you feel, then don't.
And don't police me with those questions
that I know you have in mind.
Just listen! It's time that *I* was heard.

*Why?* – that's what I want an answer to.
Why must I suffer as I do,
scrap at the bottom of the world's pile,
eking out my days in spaces
others leave?

And what's the view I have from here?
Dog eat dog, wars upon wars,
each against all -
and that is all.

'The wounded deer leaps highest.'
Did you ever hear that saying?
Cock, pure cock!

The wounded deer is a meal-in-waiting,
to be predated on;
like me, for all my life, predated on.
No, I haven't had a life, existence only.
It's time it was my time, my turn,
to be a person and to be on top.
Let someone else be me.

Why do I tell you this? Why do you listen?
You don't need to know.
You are not my keeper,
any more than I am yours.

The worm turns, and the cornered pig;
the deer kicks shit out of the wolf or lynx.
I've made a start.
He groaned the once, and sighed.
There's a lot of blood in a man, you know.
It spreads quite far.
For every stone, a pint -
I read that in a book somewhere.
He asked for it; I gave it him.
When a man's lust is up, his guard is down,
since his intelligence goes slack.
(Half the world knows this.)
That made it easy, really.
It was self-defence. I'm sure he meant me harm.

Victim no more, I thought.
As usual I was wrong.

Change? Any change to spare?
Thank you, sir, and have a lovely day.

I was in luck.
That fat bastard gave me 50p.

Victim no more - no chance, no way!
I'm victim now of fear - there's people after me -
and homelessness...
(No Fixed Abode: that's what my records say.
No-one, of No Fixed Abode,
owner of nothing, good for nothing: me!)
And sick, sick right through...
See how my hands shake.
The cure-all that I need is killing me.
(God, I could use some now!)
And poor... and lacking hope...
These - all these - close in on me.
I feel I am a hunted fox,
or rat at least.

But my wounds are deeper than dogs' teeth can go;
deeper than a surgeon's lancet ever heals;
deeper that this hell I'm sinking in.

Change?

# Tree, Bird, Fish, Bell

I saw St Mungo in a dream,
in sackcloth, driving hard a bullock cart.
With an antique camera, as he went,
the saint was shooting film.

*This is a tree that grows too fast.*
*It grows and kills.* His commentary,
about his city and its past,
he improvised, an angry text;
he growled it loud.
ZOOM to massive bole of Upas tree.
TILT up and up to swaying canopy of green.
CUT to ground where, python-like,
stout roots entwine. *It drinks too deep,*
*making the earth eviscerate and stale.*
*The overlapping lushness of its greedy leaves*
*blocks out the sun. Under the hegemony*
*of its dark rule, all lesser plants*
*have one clear course:*
*to give it room.*

CUT to images of dereliction along the Clyde.
CUT to parrot. CUT to poet. CUT to politician.
Back to parrot. BIG CLOSE-UP of open beak
and staring eye. *This is a bird*
*that chatters, and will not stop.*
*It steals the voice of others, sometimes in jest,*
*sometimes for gain, always for want*
*of proper wit.*

SLOW MIX to underwater scene:
green weed like hair; green water,
stained with oozing tributaries of red;

sleek, silver shape with grinning jaws.
*This is a fish that swims too far.*
*It eats all others, then, voracious still,*
*goes off in sharp-toothed harrying of more.*

LONG SHOT of troops in burning streets.
ZOOM to wounded, falling, dying man.
CUT to campanile, to bell, to hands on rope.
*This is a bell that tolls - unflaggingly*
*it tolls - and breaks the heart of every age,*
*ringing the knell of crafts, communities, and times,*
*speeding along the wasting of too many lives.*

I watched, still dreaming, then -
a shout! a squeal of axles! a kicking-up of dirt! -
and cart and bullock and St Mungo,
dwindling by perspective,
made a distant exit,
fast.

# Carriers

Smoke from the burning of a town rose copiously,
casually; then, ribboning and twisting in an evening breeze,
appeared to write a message in the clouds.
A woman, one of a rout of refugees, walked stumblingly,
intoning prayers or curses to the bomb-scarred ground.
Ash fell, slow blizzards.
Guns - somewhere - boomed.

Watching this latest programme on the latest war,
I felt hard questions form.
A close-up showed the woman's pain.
Captions gave in English what she mouthed:
*My daughter... Soldiers killed her...*
*I must find her... Help me... Where? ...*

She scrabbled in a field of new-turned soil,
that marked an enemy troop's advance.
First, she scrabbled with her hands;
then, to save the breaking of her nails,
she used a stone, digging, searching, moving fast
from grave to shallow and perfunctory grave.
*No. No, not here... not her...*
At the seventh disinterment: *Yes.*
*This is... This was...*
*Now I can give you proper burial...*

This way, that way,
now the unchilded woman searched a second field,
a hillside slope beyond the carnage of the first.
(Tracking in long shot, the camera stayed with her.)
Sweeping, stooping, she gathered fist-sized boulders
from the ground,
testing each in the cradle of her palm; the best
she piled to the point of spilling in a plastic pail.
Then, hidden by a tree above a winding road,
she waited till a lorry came,
conveying children from the other side.

The lorry slowed to take a bend.
As at a fairground shy, with hideous energy,
the woman aimed her random vengeance
at the children's skulls. The lorry put on speed,
but not before some hits were made.

Other women ran to her, from somewhere
that the filming did not show.
They took her pail, tipped out the boulders
that remained, and held her gently
as she stormed and cried. Together then,
with children - some were orphans, some their own -
and with a troop of animals, like them displaced by war,
in straggling file, they left the field.
Several donkeys carried loads in panniers.
To one of these, for later, different use,
with a length of washing line,
the pail was tied.

# On the Last (and Next) War

This is a war that none can win.
This is a war where sufferings for all begin.

A hostile word, or door or mind shut tight,
sets in train for years
a fear-provoking, fear-continued strife.

Attack, decry, pre-empt, avenge...
A politics of hate drags on,
with no sure end.

Who but a madman
in a woodyard in the summer's heat
starts a fire he cannot beat?

Who, when the killing fire begins to spread,
fans its flames,
and brings destruction on his head?

This is a war that leaves intact its rooted cause,
defying sense, debasing laws.

## May Day: In Parenthesis

I walked with ten thousand others on Glasgow Green;
spoke with a score; drank beer; and looked around.
Spring was well advanced; even the late reluctant ash
had opened wide its upturned leaves.
Birds, intent on nest and food, beat on the rising air.
Flurries of light petal-falls from cherry trees
marked in pink the movement of each small wind.
Since morning, clouds had sauntered off
to North and East, and left an unimpeded blue.
Balloons, in clusters, pulled, and strained,
and bobbed on upward strings.
Banners urged their many claims.

Noise was in contention all around:
singers / speakers / marchers
giving and receiving various tongue;
pipers, with their melismatic turns of tune;
a solo drummer out of sync except with self;
brass bands in a mix of different keys;
a helicopter clacking, flying - all of us as one
in adding to the richness of our May Day's sound.

*Consider well,* I heard one speaker say,
*not only where our choices lead*
*but how, with whom, and why each step along the way*
*is made. We are, or should try to be,*
*makers of the maps we follow,*
*mercators of our polity...*

*Our cause* - another orator - *has many roots.*
*Struggle feeds it. So much now, and for ever,*
*waits, weeping to be done!* ...

*Justice...*
>    *Plenty...*
(words against the epoch's grain)
>        *Progress...*
>            *Peace...*
once honoured words, and now misprized!
But, in the context of the Green, of May Day,
of our ten thousand, they took on
a more-than-usual relevance and drive.

Eurydice sang, a women's choir:
*We'll have a May Day, My O My!*
*We'll have a May Day then!* I knew the song -
by Matt McGinn - from years before, but never
had I heard it given life so longingly, so well.
*We'll join in jubilation, and the big brass band you'll hear,*
*As we march in triumph to the future with a cheer...*
At once a sadness opened up in me.
How many lives destroyed? How many more
yet doomed to go, suffering, down the ancient way?
What price - what decades put in bleak parenthesis? -
to pay for progress in our history?

Eurydice sang again, ballads in praise
of two dead giants of our foundering cause.
The one: pale-faced, hoarse-voiced,
calling on Scotland all his life to join him in his fight.
Jailed and jailed and jailed again,
his flesh but not his spirit broke.
Events appeared to leave him stuck,
misguided and misguiding in his zealousness,
but now we see he leaped ahead, prophetic,
apprehending how the century would drown the world
in deepest hell.
The other: passionate, an optimist,
convinced that everyone can contribute a mite,
or more, to all our hope's refashioning.
A soldier's rifle butt abruptly put a stop
to all her eloquence, cracking her proud head
like a coconut. But, as she foreknew,

the spirit of her work lives on.
*I was,* she said, *I am, and I shall be.*

As Eurydice sang, the thought occurred that we,
the ten thousand on the Green, and May Day marchers
everywhere, embodied Luxemburg's *shall be*.
What had we done to justify her faith,
or that of John Maclean or millions others,
who, for these our present times, made in theirs
a too-great sacrifice?
Where did we go wrong?
Where, and when, and how?
At every turn; and from the start,
matching point by point the faults of those
whose hegemony we tried to end.
Their arrogance, their partiality, their evil choice
of means - we took them for ourselves.
Our leaders, whom too trustingly we let command,
presumed too often in their mediate realms, god-like,
to rule; they dragged us down.

They stole the profit
from the produce of our lives.
They bled true meaning
from the hard-won words we use.
How can we make amends?

At my desk, writing these words, a week on,
remembering May Day,
I play cassettes to fill the silence of my room.
McGinn I play, and play again, his various songs.
One, utopian, elicits tears:
*Could you and I with fate conspire,*
*Remould this scheme of things entire,*
*Nearer to the heart's desire...*
Echoes of the Ruba'iyat beside the Clyde!
A clutch of leaflets, scattered where I dropped them,
lie across the floor.
A poster praises peace behind my chair.
A twig of cherry stripped from its tree by an earlier wind

stands near the window in a jar.
Drinking its discoloured water as it dies,
it catches, in its leaves and pale pink petals,
the last few hours of this day's shine.
Songs, leaflets, poster, twig: talismans
to aid me in my act of writing and remembering:
talismans, but failing now in power.

Confused, I hesitate at each line's wrestled end.
Hydra-headedly, my consciousness divides.
Into the widening gaps of my hiatuses,
a toil of dark invades...
But hold!
Such episodes of doubt can serve, perhaps,
as preludes and as paths to change.

# Unbending

Asylum-seekers? Yes. Their look and speech
suggest crossed seas and homelessness.
This park, a Sunday stroll, no guns, are strange;
each of the group appears bemused.
On one, the mark of hurt is cut more deep,
an older man, black-suited, strained.
He fails to note the flowers, the shrubs, the trees,
or read the labels telling when they made their passage
to this alien place of ours.

I walk here often.
There's always interest here:
winter's greening, summer's fall,
some lovely flower new out, or fruit blown down.
Today: magnolia buds.
'They're earlier this year!'
The dark-clad man looks up to face my call.
A smile, surprising him, unbends his frown.

# Scorching

*In Praise of Helen Crawfurd*


No golden mean for her, no *neither-nor,*
no coward's compromise.
It was her strength, her fate, to feel
a lack of ease
in the safety of the middle ground.
*Both-and* is what she struggled for.

Extremes of spirit and brute force
she fought with, to make them meet.
How she battered them, and bent them,
and welded them
in the heat and cunning of her work!
She sought to be and know and test all things,
and pushed them, and herself, beyond
the breaking point.

From out the fracture in her soul
there leaped a scorching flame of life.

## Seed-corn

*Seeds For the Planting Shall Not Be Ground Up:*
so Kathe Kollwitz called a picture that she made.
It shows three children hugged within the circle
of their mother's arms; the mother fiercely
and with vigilance looks round,
their guard.

Such love the wise extend to more than family
and to seeds.

Thoughts for the thinking shall not be let to slide;
values for our saving shall not be lightly held,
nor scorned;
books for the reading shall not be pulped,
nor put in skips, nor thrown on fires
and burned.

# Spiderlike

Building & rebuilding,
over & over where unmaking reigns,
always from love, for love,
how we labour
to remake the ravelled world a home;
& how in anger we relearn,
always & again from scratch,
the need for love
as home & world that we build up
repeatedly are smashed

                         & & &

# A Fish Rising

*'The path to the future is one of unavoidable defeat...'*
Rosa Luxemburg

*From the bottom of an ancient pool,*
*said to be bottomless,*
*up to the film of its meeting with the still air,*
*hungry, in search of fly or grub,*
*a fat carp rises.*
*With a barbed kiss,*
*it breaks the surface and the silence*
*of this summer's day, and eats;*
*then, glidingly, it noses*
*back to the cool of its brown deep,*
*a world away.*

Romans in their heyday were the first
to stock this pool. Thereafter, monks
hymning their dead and risen god
tended the fish, until in turn
their fortunes, like the Romans',
fell.

Now, at another epoch's ruined end,
the world in flames,
I pace the footworn path around the pool.
Heavy with thought,
I count the failed resurgences
that history has seen,
brief flowerings of the people's will.
They grew wild, their early promise
of a new-style beauty
unremembered now, or else despised.

I wonder at the paradox of change:
the pulling-down, as if by Samson
in the temple of the Philistines,
of forms of polity that have plagued the weak,

while upstart oligarchs,
no less appetitive and cruel than those deposed,
creep in.

Time upon time, the ancient dream
of plenty's peace has died;
and yet succeeding calvaries along the way
may serve as school and seed
of future victory.

We are as one with the silent work of earthworms
in their fining of the soil.
We are - or might become - a force more powerful
than rivers' wearing-down of mountains
to a peneplain.
We find fit emblem and a parallel
in each year's fattening and embrowning
of its fields of grain.

One speck of dirt, or gold,
can tip the heaviest-laden balance
from the straight. (Taking hope,
I count some auguries of hope.) One fact,
discrepant with the dogma of the orthodox,
can breach its errors' edifice, admitting light.
One wound, one cry, one song, one name
can travel faster than a Caesar's hate.

*I see a movement in the pool,*
*a glimpse of mottle, a sun-reflecting curve,*
*a twist of tail. Slowly,*
*the carp begins once more to stir.*
*Beyond, beneath, I strain*
*to see the bottom of the pool's brown deep,*
*but fail.*

# The People's Palace History Paintings

From their random streets of suffering
they entered history, and sheered the chain
that bound them to their epoch
and their narrow fate.
The space for freedom
that by force of will they opened up
remains for us to enter, and re-win.
Their lives' example burns,
sticking in our consciences, reproachfully,
like sulphur flames.

Ken Currie's art compacts in striking paint
the hurt, intelligence, tenacity, and hope
that fired at first the Calton Weavers,
then the Chartists, Suffragettes, and Socialists.
Each in their own hard time,
they dared assert against the partialities
of class and state
their universal claim.

As in a dream of hell,
so in the artist's use of colour
darker tones predominate.
The imagined source of light -
a loom on fire, a foundry, miners' lamps,
or, distantly, a burst of sunrise
struggling through impeding clouds - picks out,
amid the toil and welter of his scenes,
a choice of images that tell our tale:

there, from two hundred years ago,
the scarlet cap and tree of Liberty;
next, the slogans *Fight or Starve,*
*Weave Trust With Truth, Fear Not;*
then Maclean, the teacher's and accuser's
pointing finger,

his battered globe, and blackboard proofs;
and, in our present age, in final prominence,
emerging from the problematic of the past,
a flag, unfurling,
held by age-instructed youth.

# Fighting Back

'This is me,' she said, lurching, smiling,
'road-testing my new leg, a wee bit extra every day.'
She slapped her thigh - plastic, maybe; maybe steel -
then told me, 'Life's a pig, the way it's shafted me.
But I'm fighting back, you know. Oh, yes!'
Her aim, as she explained: to walk once more
the route she marched, with others, long years past,
the whole road South, to Parliament, *For Jobs Not War*.

The woman pursed her lips and frowned -
in pain? in prayer? - then into gear, and off!
As if a drunkard on the heave and ho
of some ship's deck, she staggered fast
to where a side street was.  There,
puffed, at the corner, turning back, she paused
and gave two signs:
a thumbs-up, then clenched fist.

# In Brecht's Bar

'The Hollow Mountain? Ever heard of it?'
He placed his glass next ours, then -
'Seat taken? No.' - sat down.
'I overheard you talking.
Seems History's your thing. Mine, too;
though all the dates and names that interest me
are never put in any books at all.'
His face was strong, the likeness caught, soon after,
in a painting, hung now on the bar-room wall.

The big man spoke with us, an hour or more,
of tunnelling:
of howking out the heart of Cruachan
when he was young,
to hold the dynamo that feeds the country
power.

Now dead, he is a part himself - a hero -
in the History he liked to hear.

# Giving Back Riches

*In Praise of Paul Robeson*


Experience showed him a world divided;
in his song he held it whole.
Carrying a deep wound, his and the world's,
dreaming a generous dream, he was a giant,
serving the people.
Few neared the strength of his standing.
In their many tongues, he spoke for the poor,
giving back riches.
Against wrong, with his life, all his life,
he waged war; he was unbeaten.
He is remembered in Glasgow.
He gave us his sword and balm.
His echo lingers, loud
for those with souls to hear,
singing the world sane.

# Granny Albyn's Complaint

Bugs and rats do well, and the occasional crook.
Once, the mister bigs of politics came here, to win some votes.
Not now; no point.

Were you to look,
what hellscape do you think my window shows?
There's a knot-hole in the nailed-on wood, down low.
Stoop, and you'd get an evil eyeful,
worse when a wind blows.
Right now, you'd see the usual needles dropped around;
a splat of vomit; a sprinkled, sticky, bloody trail.
God knows what knifed or battered hardman staggered past,
in pain.
Strong they go, and weak return.

The masterminds who dumped us in this no-man's-land,
require us here.
Lengthening the odds against us, they cut short our lives.
Casually they do it, by proxy or default.
Our loss; their gain.

Was it for this our species heaved from out the slime,
stood up, and looked, and walked;
found speech, made tools,
and learned to manage nature's things, and space, and time?
Was it for this our builders-up of culture lived,
and, struggling, made their billion-hearted sacrifice?
Self-knowledge and self-rule we've failed to learn.
Fools, we strut, or slave.
Bare-arsed baboons show better sense:
their worst aggressions are curtailed by simple rules.
But we...!

The world's well-being is the victim of our arrogance.
Whole habitats lie ruined in our wars of greed.
The seed-corn we would sow depletes, through negligence.

I am an exile from the country of our past.
Where once we made our home, now deer range, or sheep;
and bracken showers its smothering spores.
Cities took us; continents we filled.
We bear with us a load of memories where we go:
names and longings, beauties, horrors, fears...

I am an exile also from the future we had hoped to build,
where peace in many tongues might sing,
and plenty wipe out want, with even hand.
Slim chance!
Easier to scatter than to gather in!

Amphibians -
feet in the muck, eyes searching for a source of light -
that's what we are,
our hard-won lives held cheap.
And yet the cost of living in our ghetto soars:
just keeping going is a worsening fight.

I have the knack - the luck -
in my eye's mind, to bring to view
the best and most of Scotland in this little room.
Sometimes, as a helicopter might, I soar
from Solway's mud, coast-hugging West and North, to
Shetland's stacks,
then South again by East-coast capes and firths.
New routes I look for overland -
following fault-lines; river-running; hopping peak to peak -
charting as I go, as if an alpinist,
unclimbed - unclimbable? - new ice- and rock-ascents.

As if a painter, too, I gaze on skyline sweeps,
and wonder how to capture Cruachan or Lochnagar
or Beinn Etcetera
in art.

Bridges, dams, and towers, I conjure up,
and parks, and streets, and city squares...
wherever builders' heart and head and eye and hand

have worked together well.
There's much to revel in:
not here, not now, but virtual, you understand!

I'll tell you what I want: to walk -
I'd need new hips and heart -
to walk right out this hole,
by way of every place I know, from Aa to Unst;
to walk, and sing, and see a Wood of Caledon grow up,
bigger/greener than it was before;
to see a land re-built, a peopled land;
to gather friends around, and friends of friends,
and, Deborah-like, make captive our captivity,
put right our wrongs.

My complaint?
What was mine is taken from me, lost, or wrecked!

In my own home, homeless!
It's Scotland's ancient curse.
But, no ebb-tide ever ran without its following flood.
Cha tainig traich gun mhuir-lan 'na deidh.
Be sure of it:
my vision will, sometime, assume the flesh of fact.

# Boogying

*In Praise of Nelson Mandela*

Cold, grey; the sky teems.
*Umbrellas down!*
He's here, Mandela's here -
in Glasgow - free!
Quietly, the hero speaks,
spelling out with care his strategy for change.
We watch, listen, disregarding rain.
*Umbrellas down!*
We want - all thousands of us want -
to see our history-in-making clear.

Then, as singers on his platform
start to sing, he dances.
Mandela boogies in George Square.
We boogy, and - *Nkosi Sikelel' iAfrica* -
we all give voice to their proud song.

Hope today finds hope,
which Africa, for all our sakes,
kept strong.

# Various

*In Praise of Matt McGinn*

A rough, rough voice, expressive
of tenderness, as of comedy, as of grief
or anger at the world's great wrongs;
a body packed with vigour;
conviction absolute - these
were his traits.

He was various, as Glasgow is.

A ship, skilled work of hands,
of years, of thought, of pride,
fitted out and raring for the trials of sea;
the sometimes troubled waters of his soul;
lessons learned and told from Scotland's
and the world's hard history;
the Clyde, and all who know it,
not for one moment slackening,
not standing still;
sun rising, moon rising, hope rising;
jokes, giants, cuddles, teabreaks,
yo-yos, football, ghosts... all things,
the real, imagined, and surreal: a treasure chest
for us to share, richer than a heaping to the highest stars
of selfish gold: a glittering
of active mind: a store of loving care - such
were the substance of his songs.

He was big, as Glasgow is.

# Glasgow's Needleworks Project

Stand back, well back.
Enjoy the clash of hues, more splendid
than the Northern Lights, or peacock's tail!
The chemistry of dyes
finds here a worthy showcase for its skills.
Patched, stuck on, embroidered, scribed,
light-hearted fruit of many hours,
how well these dozen hangings put the case
for Glasgow's genius,
and tell the story of the city's year!

Some would have us see things
through a smoke-grimed glass,
discerning only darker shades of monochrome.
There is a ready cure for such negaters:
to look at and to learn from
these our brighter-than-Bayeux tapestries;
to look at, learn from, and to borrow
something of their brilliance of fire.

Now come close,
and focus on whatever details
hold the trackings of your curious eye: -

In January, perhaps, a rage of shoppers,
storming in a burst of buying
through the stores;

in April, in a park, the flowering
of a show of gaudy clothes,
flamboyantly put on by old and young
in honour of a sky of birds;

in May, against a field of red,
black-coated workers, marching;
on their banner,
her arms as muscled as a titan's hams,

a May Day figure - spirit? goddess? sister? -
roundly stating terms;

or, in June, a juggler, Siva-like,
a nurse-mechanic-teacher-cleaner-driver-cook
et cetera - a mother in her multiplicity
of roles...

What else?

a dragonfly, an optimist,
hatched out, and launched on shimmering wings,
three months at least before due time;

skylines, at rose-pink dawn
and orange-tawny dusk,
showing in hard-edged silhouette
our city's built magnificence;

a Paisley-pattern tree, its roots revealed,
traceable to soils both West and East;

and, in all the months,
unchanging through the seasons'
as through lives' and epochs' flux,
a steady band of river packed with ships.

# Chorus of the Masses
## Against the Elites

We are the nothings you walk past.
Your lowest and least,
we live in the margins of your power.

Expendable, we fight your many wars.
Your triumphs we pay for,
but have none.

Unheeded and unnamed,
we make your schemes come true.

Every ton and inch and cubic yard and chisel-cut
of every building you command,
is ours.
Every furrow ploughed and filled with seed
is ours.
Your wealth-producing factories;
your cities -
ours!

Day in, day out, we do your work and will.
We pipe the water that you need from reservoir to tap;
we stitch the clothes that cover up your nakedness;
we bake the bread (and cake) you eat.

We are your numerous and essential kin.
Suffering most, we learn most.
Our slave-songs make symphonies;
our longings, creeds.

We dig your graves.

# Scum

I stepped from a landing stage
into a skiff moored there.
At once, the boat appeared to come alive.
No need for oars:
self-propelled, we moved upstream.
I felt the bang and running of the river as,
against the flow, we hammered hard.
Faster we moved, always faster.
Behind us, rippling and rolling, our wake unfurled.
We ventured on, into a stretch of unknown land,
until we came to where, on either side,
a shade of willows dipped and trailed. Here,
the river broadened, and the current slowed.
Suddenly, we stopped, held by no anchor,
but by some secret power.
A hand, huge, out of all proportion to the scene,
out of the sky, pushed down.
It swept the canopy of the trees aside,
and, cleaving through a patch of surface scum,
plunged to the river's bottom at our side.
The fingers trawled, flickering, pale.
Then, quickly, into a burst of sunlight, into air,
the hand scooped up and out, and held on high
a spluttering, kicking, snatched-from-drowning soul.
Who he was, or she, I could not tell;
nor whose the saving hand.
Before the dream dissolved, two facts impinged:
first, that everything I saw began as monochrome,
but in the sun acquired a strongly coloured sheen;
second, that the scabby cap of scum upon the pool
was shown to be a sheet, a floating, crumpled sheet,
incongruous, of beaten gold.

# May Day: Happy Returns

Night.
At my window, breathing in fresh air,
I smell the raw earth of my potato patch,
wet from the downpour of a full day's rain.
The clouds' dense grey has cleared,
revealing stars. Tangled in the foliage
of my neighbour's chestnut tree,
like Christmas lights,
they complement the candles of its flowers.
I look, admire,
and note the luminosity of the sky's late blue.
Even after dusk and setting,
slantiways, the sun can touch us
with its after-glow.
But cold! It's getting cold.
I put a jersey on; reach for some Scotch;
and drink; and...

*Dong.* A tenor bell.
Its sound is carried from a church
some streets away, its ringing
riding on the current of a freshening wind.
Eleven o'clock. Suddenly,
it seems that Glasgow Green is riding, too.
Detached from where it lies -
has lain since Clyde first flowed -
it hurtles fast, airborne, across the town.
Now, dwindling through my window,
it broadens out beneath me where I stand.
I keep my balance; look around.
Fifty May Days, counting this one,
I have marched with others here;
was here, rain-soaked, this afternoon.

In a rush, in a surge, in a leap of love,
my thoughts reach out -
if they were arms, they would hug tight -

to gather-in time-sundered and far-distant friends.
And more: in this, my harvesting of love,
I hunger also for the friends of friends.
As I wish, so, from their respective years
and quarters of the globe, they come.
They smile; they greet me with their eyes.
And some are dead, I see, and some not born.
No matter! One by one, each with a torch,
a various, equal band, happily they glide
and join me, making as they do
a galaxy of light and kindness on the Green.

A mound of turf heaves up.
Daisies, flowering instantly, gleam white.
Figures, famous and admired, step out.
First, the writers Gray and Spence,
cartographers of Glasgow's multiverse.
They turn Mozartians for a while, and sing the parts
of Papageno and Tamino from *The Magic Flute*.
At their singing, energy alike from evil
as from good is tamed.
Glasgow's birdlife, predators and prey,
are moved by curiosity to leave their roosts;
they flock to be a front-row audience.
Amid the whirring of their wings,
our city's epic artist, Currie, comes to paint;
the Scottish Colourists are at his side.
For his green, at the instigation
of these tutor-friends, he dips his brush
in the sap of juicy stalks and leaves of grass.
For his yellow, he blends the pollen of the catkin
and the ore of gold. For his silver,
he takes the scales of leaping salmon
in the Clyde; for his blue,
the skies of furthest space commingled with the petals
of self-heal; and for his purple, heather.

Kafka, too, is here.
(I love and dread his *Castle* and his *Trial*.)
He comes on stage, and with him,

though they never met in life,
his Scots translator, Edwin Muir.
They choose to sing the roles of Mozart's priests,
but soon they switch: Kafka to bar-room ballads,
Muir to hymns of Eden lost and found.
Still the priestly music is maintained -
James Watt takes up the theme.
Here it was, when walking on the Green,
that he conceived the steam-condenser
that would change the world.
Now it is steam organs that preoccupy his mind.
Before us, as we listen, as we watch,
a giant one appears. This organ's pipes outvoice
the largest orchestra and massed mixed choir.
With gravity, the engineer lets rip.
Even the deaf can hear, including one,
shock-haired and grim of face, who is inspired
to stretch and coil the gleaming trumpet
of his hearing aid, and put a mouthpiece in.
Puffing out his cheeks, he blows.
Out pours a brassy, brilliant rag.
All turn, entranced; we clap.
It is a rare, impromptu treat. Beethoven: it is him,
the trombonist Ian Menzies at his side,
John Cairns (piano) at the rear!
He's with the Clyde Valley Stompers,
a jazzman for the night.

A football game starts up.
It ranges back and forth, from Clyde to Forth,
at thunder- if not lightning-speed.
But, strange! there is no ball.
Instead, the players, hundreds of them, use
the rounded, golden, lovely notes
the Stompers plentifully provide.
Here's one, a middle C on clarinet, from Forrie Cairns.
It's taken up by Kitchenbrand, 'The Rhino',
arch-blooterer of goals, returned to us from decades
sitting out in no-man's-team.
The note is passed from him to Thornton,

a headerer of skill;
and now to Johnstone, full of jinks,
him of the Einstein space-and-time-defying feet.
What runs! What riffs!

This multiplex of music, thickening in its harmony
beyond the dreams of many Bachs,
maintains its polyphonic progress
on and on; and on...
*Boom. Boom. Boom.*
A triple note, triple forte, halts our concert
in its tracks.
It is Mozart, striking with a billiard cue upon a gong.
*Boom. Boom. Boom.*
A second triplet, a twelve-tone row
percussively compressed, now follows hard.
We look, and see our own dear minstrel,
Matt McGinn.
His instrument: a twelve-string amplified guitar.
*Boom. Boom. Boom.*
Two drums this time, two drummers
clad in the costume of *The Magic Flute*'s Armed Men.
One of them I recognise at once.
I know his features from Ken Currie's art:
our vision-holding Moses, John Maclean.
The second drummer is myself.

Silence now - *lunga pausa* -
packed with meaning, as in a score
composed by Scotland's world-embracing and world-
honoured Ronald Stevenson.
He's here - I spot his neat white dagger of a beard -
a prophet in his land.

Now, from his daisy mound above our heads,
the boyish Mozart, angel-tongued, orates:
*Please,* he says, *do not embarrass me,*
*you who perform my* Magic Flute,
*or improvise on themes from it.*
*I am two hundred years more wise*

*than when, a creature of my times, I wrote the work,*
*and let gross errors taint its plot, evil clustering*
*round the female, and the lowly-born, and black.*

At this confession, cataracts of voices,
louder than the Falls of Clyde in spate,
in ragged overlap shout out:
*aana koia, aw aw, ayo, bali, be-enii* and *da;*
and *igen, io, evet, krahpkahk, na'am,* and *ne-eh,*
and *jow,* and *vahng,* and *yes,*
and other terms in other tongues, unknown to me,
too numerous for me to guess.
James Joyce jumps up, inspirer (awe-inspirer)
of huge tribes of bards.
A multi-lingual pile of grammars and thesauruses,
stacked with care to form a ziggurat, supports him
to a dizzying height.
He laughs his pleasure at the cocktail sound
that all these shouted affirmations make.

Of a sudden, a juddering shakes the Green.
The earth's rotation has been stopped.
Hills, in a faster fit of orogenesis
than geology describes, rise up, snow-topped.
Rivers, running deeply, find a common course.
We have a landscape now, new-formed,
to suit a city's redevelopment.
A choice of buildings, felled then fetched,
strangely with no dirt or din, from many lands,
are intermixed with our own best.
Streets, according to a pleasing plan, combining aspects
of the East and West, the modern and the old,
are opened up and filled with folk.
Trees, of every size and age and sort,
are planted as a screen on either hand.
Their perfumed blossoms multi-colouredly unfold.
Statues of war-mongers and the oppressive rich
begin to totter, crack, reduce to rubble, now to dust.
A light rain falls, and the wind blows warm.
The dust converts to clay; the clay to children,

those whom history has damaged in its passing by.
Crammed full with life, they race like suns,
whole and happy, in the torchlight
of our Glasgow night.

What's this? What next?
A second juddering, greater than the first!
The earth resumes its turning, but, oddly, in reverse.
We find it hard to stand.
We hold each other, mutual anchors, mutual stays.
Thoughts we have that weaken us, or shame us,
now we feel constrained to re-examine and to fix.
Into the intentness of this labour,
a voice (half-strange, half-known) comes ringing in.
At this, the earth's rotation self-corrects.

*What of those, the uncountable, the discounted,*
*those whose deaths and lives have gained them*
*no memorial...?*
So the voice begins,
weighing us, and finding wanting.
*I look for them but cannot find the heroes*
*and the heroines who, unknown to us,*
*made deserts green, turned stones to bread,*
*and bread to song;*
*who crafted every tool with which we work;*
*who used their knowledge of the properties*
*of earth and water, air and fire*
*to conjure culture out of Nature's stubbornness.*
*They should be here as honoured guests.*
*And where are those who took the sounds of speech,*
*like pebbles in a burn, and polished them,*
*till they had shaped a language fit for various use?*
*And where are those who tended young or sick or old,*
*or were themselves the subject of another's care?*
*And where are those who had no chance*
*to make their mark, who could do nothing*
*but survive a little space against the odds,*
*sufficient task?*

Who is this voice of challenge and remembering?
Is it Red Rosa Luxemburg? No.
She is too busy handing theses to the crowd.
Still bloodied from the blow that killed her,
she wears a large brimmed hat to hide the wound.
Even Heaven cannot heal her
while her died-for cause is incomplete.
Nor is it Hildegard, precursor of the Greens;
nor Thenew, mother of the city's patron saint.
They, sisters, move elsewhere,
deep in their study and their gentleness.

The voice cries out again: *Let's see
and hear you now!* summoning her forgotten
and her dear despised. Responsive to the call,
from every furthest settlement and age,
a rush of millions comes. By a miracle,
there is room enough for them to join us here,
and space besides. Some of the arrivals sing,
some speak, some dance in wild or stately steps,
some show their skill with needle,
hammer, shovel, pen, computer,
or a myriad other tools of their respective trades.
All bring a showing-forth of their identities,
and share them with all others in this carnival
that we have here. Among them, Eddie Morgan
is at work, his eye, and ear, and intellect,
as always, at full stretch; he moves like mercury
from group to group, camcorder running.
Glasgow's Poet Laureate, he'll make sure our carnival
survives, its every quiddity set down in published print.
Although so many languages are used,
although so many musics, dramas, lifeworks,
and philosophies contend,
no babel but a pentecost occurs -
no hodge-podge dissonance, but patternings of patterns,
where all opposites in good order are composed.
I add my bit.

But hold! At hyphen, comma, colon, semicolon,
or the middle of a step or act or bar,
upon the toot of random passing hooter,
all these marvels cease.
My crammed encounters fade.
My room shrinks back to normal size.
Real time returns.
What time?

Confused, I check my watch.
Approaching twelve: so late, so soon!
I reach once more for whisky; pour one last, large glass.
*To absent friends!* - I drink a silent toast -
*and all-including commonwealth!*

*Dong.* Streets away,
the churchbell starts its midnight chimes.
I draw my curtains,
and shut out the chestnut tree and sky of stars.
Tired, content, I muse...
Books, and smell of soil, and history,
and friends, and movements of the earth,
and magic transformations,
and far, far travellings of my mind,
and hosts of arts and trades, and flowers, and torches,
and the world in Glasgow Green,
have in one short hour, in lavish measure,
made me strong.
I am lucky: filled, fulfilled,
and greatly charged with change.
My five senses and my soul, like mountain thunder,
like a plucked string, in jubilation
hum and roll and ring.
On this note, this dominant,
rememoried, reoriented, and renewed,
I count my sum of blessings,
and conclude.

# Bread and Book

*Take this bread,*
they said, our ancient wise.
The others, strangers, took and ate,
surprised that friendship met them
on an alien shore.

*Take this book,*
they later said, these strangers
settled here. We took, and read,
and made their alien words our own,
which tell of bread and wisdom,
and of friendship
on an ancient and familiar shore.

# Athene

Great reasoner, great justicer,
your qualities are needed now,
now as never. Bereaved, bereaving,
in the world's long round of hydra-headed hate,
we are bleeding in our tribal wars,
or wasting day on day in famine, flood,
or drought.

Goddess of the bridle and the look-out post,
the map, the rudder, and the keel,
you are our olive-bringer, tamer of furies,
inspirer of our commonweal.

You know the places where true wisdom lies;
with your familiars, you go down deep.
As through timber with a sharp-edged heavy blade,
you cleave through habit where it counsels wrong,
but have restraint. Backwards you think,
and forwards, checking the rash first deed.

Projection on divinity of our human best,
Athene, kindly one, sustain us,
and instruct!

# The Net

Take a map or globe,
and, with imagined pencil,
rule the line of force that runs between us,
soul to soul.

Go on and draw, with you as hub,
the sum of spoking radii
that plot your other reachings-out
and warm returns of love.

Suppose that I,
and all our many-membered company,
have done the same,
and that we bring our friendships' interlinks
within one overlapping scheme.

What large geometries are here,
thickening and neat!
How long before they spread
to catch and hold and heal,
across both miles and years,
the world complete?

# Heavensayings

*Words of Experience Spoken by Some Inhabitants of Purgatory*

1. The wind in the hollies is different from the wind in the willows; the song of the willow warbler is different from that of the sedge warbler - as different as Schubert's art is from Fats Waller's. Long live all such particularities!

2. Look carefully and you will see a pale-green chevron, one of the most beautiful things in the world, on each of the three leaves of a clover; or four, if you are lucky. The oftener you look, the luckier you get.

3. *Cooee* is an Australian Aboriginal word. It is the word that travellers call out again and again as they go further and further into the bush. It means, *I am here*, and requires someone friendly, not too distant, to hear it. There are many other words like this, in all languages, to be learned and listened to.

4. The sort of elegance that engineers routinely achieve, as in the design and fabrication of ships' propellers, has yet to be approached in the field of politics. We are working on it.

5. Whitman's amplitude is a thing worth having. *Within me latitude widens,* he roared, *and longitude lengthens... Within me is the longest day.*

6. Innovators need conservers. The rare plant in a dwindling peat-bog may hold the germ of a medical or agricultural advance.

7. Digging the ground and lobbing communication satellites into the air - just two of the things that people do that make the human species human. How many others? The act of naming should itself be included in any count.

8. In West Africa, at least in fables, there are certain deer that crouch down and blow the sand from each other's eyes when a desert storm is blowing about them.

9. *Love's not Time's fool.* Whoever said that said something important.

10. Some people go past closed doors assuming that they are all locked against them. But others, the optimists, cannot pass doors without trying them. After a certain number of knob-turnings, they reckon, one will surely open to them.

11. *Driven... drawn... again... towards... together... on... beyond...* These seven words make a poem, an epic, which might be called 'The History and Future of Humankind'.

12. Thoreau lived and worked and died in the belief that *the roots of the huckleberries may survive till the woods are cut again.* He was probably right.

# No Mean City

Here songs break out more frequently by far
than fights,
while jokes, debates with strangers, affirmations,
and confessions
are a commonplace.
Here no home for the unseeing stare,
for cold uncaring.
No.
Our spoken and unspoken rules require:
*communicate and celebrate.*

Enjoy the musics of our many-times-repeated emphases,
as, shuttling on our loom of words,
we come up sharp at our extremes,
reverse
and then with passion or panache
fly back!

Enjoy! Participate!
Add to our criss-crossings of experience
your own brave counterpoint!
Here is no home for the unseeing stare,
for cold uncaring;
here no hiding for the po- or poker-face.
With our whole selves, hotly,
we communicate,
and celebrate.

# A Wishing Tree

*Green Thoughts in a Red Shade*

A May Day every day.
*Clean air, clean politics, clean sweeps.*
Teachers who learn; leaders who follow.
*A second chance.*
A first chance.
*To have known sooner what we know now.*
A whole-body transplant, and a new mind.
*Helping hands.*
Enough.
*Fair shares.*
One day free.
*'The wings of the dove...'*
More answers to more questions.
*No need to wish.*
No end of wishing.

# NOTES

### A New Mask Of Anarchy
Goya's *Los Caprichos* was published in 1799. The best known of these prints is *The Sleep of Reason* : 'Imagination deserted by Reason begets monsters. United with Reason, she is mother of all the arts, and the source of their marvels.'

### Auguries Of Evil
The first part of this poem borrows from William Blake's 'London'.

### Tree, Bird, Fish, Bell
The City of Glasgow's coat-of-arms features a tree, in which a bird perches, a fish holding a ring in its mouth, and a bell. These emblems relate to events in the life of Glasgow's patron saint, St Kentigern, also known as Mungo. The tree gave the saint a frozen branch from which he was able to conjure fire. The bird was a dead robin, into which he breathed new life. The fish and the ring were crucial to a bit of peace-making that he undertook between a murderous king and a queen, operating very much on the queen's side. The bell was a gift from Rome to Glasgow. There is an oddly negative jingle associated with the coat-of-arms which every Glasgow schoolchild learns. One version of it goes:

> *This is the tree that never grew.*
> *This is the bird that never flew.*
> *This is the fish that never swam.*
> *This is the bell that never rang.*

### May Day: In Parenthesis
Glasgow Green is a large public park on the North bank of the River Clyde. The People's Palace, occupying part of the Green, is a museum of social history, opened in 1898. Eurydice is a socialist women's choir, so called because it is not the Orpheus Choir, which went before it. Matt McGinn (1928-77) was a singer-songwriter, political activist and much else besides. Rosa Luxemburg (1870-1919) and John Maclean (1879-1923)

were Marxist revolutionaries who gave their lives to struggle, sharing a particular concern for peace and internationalism. At his trial for sedition in Edinburgh in 1918, Maclean famously said, 'I am not here as the accused. I am here as the accuser of capitalism, dripping with blood from head to foot.'

### Scorching
Helen Crawfurd (1877-1954) contributed greatly to the struggles for women's suffrage, peace, internationalism, fair rents, social justice, etc., from the time of the First World War right up to her death. She was active in the Women's Social and Political Union, the Women's Peace Crusade, the Independent Labour Party, and later, the Communist Party of Great Britain.

### Seed-corn
Kathe Kollwitz (1867-1945) was a German artist, whose works protested against war, poverty and injustice.

### Spiderlike
This poem borrows from Adrienne Rich's 'Natural Resources', which describes watching a spider building its web.

### The People's Palace History Paintings
Ken Currie's series of eight History Paintings are on display in the People's Palace, on Glasgow Green. Commissioned to mark the bicentenary of the massacre of the Calton Weavers, Scotland's first trade union martyrs, they tell the story of the Labour Movement up to, and beyond, the Miners Strike of 1984-5.

### In Brecht's Bar
In 'A Worker Reads History' Bertolt Brecht asked, 'In the evening when the Great Wall of China was finished / Where did the masons go?

### Giving Back Riches
Paul Robeson (1898-1976) visited Glasgow several times between the 1930s and 60s, the last occasion being when he sang at the May Day rally in Queen's Park in 1964.

**Granny Albyn's Complaint**
The Wood of Caledon once covered a large part of Scotland. For Deborah, see Judges, chapters 4 and 5.

**Boogying**
This poem celebrates the day (9 October, 1993) when Nelson Mandela came to Glasgow to receive the Freedom of the City.

**Glasgow's Needleworks Project**
'Keeping Glasgow in Stitches' was a community tapestry project undertaken in 1990. It comprises twelve banners, one for each month of the year, and celebrates aspects of everyday life in the city.

**May Day: Happy Returns**
Alasdair Gray and Alan Spence are writers whose works include novels, short stories, plays, poems and essays. Gray is also an artist. His novel *Lanark* (1981) and Spence's novel *The Magic Flute* (1990) inspired several of the poems in this book. Edwin Muir (1887-1959) was a poet, novelist, and critic. Edwin Morgan was Glasgow's first Poet Laureate (1999-2002). The Scottish Colourists were Samuel Peploe (1871-1935), John Duncan Fergusson (1874-1961), Leslie Hunter (1877-1931), and Francis Cadell (1883-1937). Don Kitchenbrand and Willie Thornton played for Rangers; Jimmy 'Jinkie' Johnstone played for Celtic. Hildegard of Bingen (1098-1139) was an abbess, artist, botanist, philosopher, physician, poet, and theologian as well as a composer of music. St Thenew was the mother of Glasgow's patron saint, St Kentigern (or Mungo). Ronald Stevenson is a composer, pianist, author and teacher.

**No Mean City**
The title of the poem is borrowed from the (in)famously dark novel by Alexander McArthur and H. Kingsley Long (1935). An alternative title might be *Dear Green Place*, borrowed from the late Archie Hind's masterpiece of 1966.